About this book

Old hags gather round a smoking cauldron; they are shouting incantations as they toss one more newt's leg into the boiling brew. Evil spirits are conjured up from thin air; ghoulish creatures rise up out of the stinking marshes, while, high overhead, the woman in black flies by on her broomstick.

This is the picture that immediately springs to mind when we think of witchcraft and magic. But there is much more to it than that. There is ritual magic—a human sacrifice to the gods in return for their good-will. There is fortune-telling—peering into the future and forecasting what will happen in the years to come. Then there is spiritualism or talking with the dead!

This book covers all sorts of witchcraft and magic. It explains what magic means, and the different ways it was practised throughout history. It also tells of modern magic—of palmistry and poltergeists, of seances and crystal balls; the Druids of Stonehenge and the rain-makers of Africa are all in this book. Read on, if you dare!

Some of the words printed in *italics* may be new to you. You can look them up in the list on page 93.

AN EYEWITNESS HISTORY BOOK

Witchcraft and Magic

PAT HODGSON

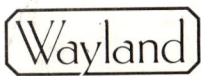

More Eyewitness History Books

The Railway Builders   Alistair Barrie
Pirates and Buccaneers   Tilla Brading
The Mayflower Pilgrims   Brenda Colloms
The Age of Drake   Leonard Cowie
Children of the Industrial Revolution   Penelope Davies
Country Life in the Middle Ages   Penelope Davies
Markets and Fairs   Jane Dorner
Newgate to Tyburn   Jane Dorner
Kitchens and Cooking   Kathy & Mike Eldon
The Story of the Cinema   Helen du Feu
The Story of the Wheel   Peter Hames
Men in the Air   Roger Hart
Popular Entertainment   Elizabeth Holt
A Victorian Sunday   Jill Hughes
Livingstone in Africa   Denis Judd
Stagecoach and Highwayman   Stephanie McKnight
The Tudor Family   Ann Mitchell
The Horseless Carriage   Lord Montagu
The Firefighters   Ann Mountfield
The Slave Trade   Ann Mountfield
Clothes in History   Angela Schofield
Florence Nightingale   Philippa Stewart
Sport through the Ages   Peter Wilson
The Glorious Age of Charles II   Helen Wodzicka
Ships and Seafarers   Helen Wodzicka
The Printer and his Craft   Helen Wodzicka
Road Transport   Susan Goldblatt
Shops and Shopping   Ann Mountfield
Shakespeare and his Theatre   Philippa Stewart
Tutankhamun's Egypt   Penelope Davies & Philippa Stewart
The Story of Medicine   Kathy & Mike Eldon
Toys in History   Angela Schofield
Tom-tom to Television   Kathy & Mike Eldon
Animals in War   Pat Hodgson
Islam   Brenda Ralph Lewis
Overland to the West   Pat Hodgson
Street Cries   Patricia Morrell
Steam Engines   Brenda Ralph Lewis
When Dinosaurs Ruled   Brenda Ralph Lewis
Greek Myth and Legend   Brenda Ralph Lewis
Beads, Barter and Bullion   Brenda Ralph Lewis

Frontispiece   The witches from Shakespeare's *Macbeth*

ISBN 0 85340 618 9
Copyright © 1978 by Wayland Publishers Limited
First published in 1978 by Wayland Publishers Limited
49 Lansdowne Place, Hove, East Sussex.
BN3 1HF, England
Printed and bound in the UK by   Morrison and Gibb Limited, Edinburgh

Contents

1 Ritual Magic 7
2 Witches and Demons 29
3 Looking into the Future 49
4 Raising the Dead 67
New Words 93
More Books 94
Index 95

1. Ritual Magic

Magic is an attempt to change the natural laws of the universe and it is as old as the human race. We all use magic *rituals* today, but now we call them superstitions or "old wives' tales". Every mascot carried into the examination room is a good-luck charm. We touch wood, cross our fingers, avoid walking under ladders and read *horoscopes* in the newspapers. For early magicians the rules of magic were like the laws of science. A spell had to be followed exactly if it was to work. Imagine what would happen if a scientist mixed dangerous chemicals together in an experiment. There might be an equally explosive result if the right formula was not used in a spell.

The magic practised by the first sorcerors was very simple. They believed that magical control could be reached by mimicry, so they copied the actions of animals and birds. The Indian magician, shown opposite, is pretending to be a bird. His hands are in a flying position and there is a dead bird in his hair. The otter skin on his belt contains magical charms. He is a medicine man of the Algonquin Indians of Canada. They believed birds carried messages between the earth and the spirits.

HORN DANCE. Some of the earliest magical *rituals* were to do with hunting. The Abbots Bromley Horn Dancers in the picture above are performing a prehistoric dance supposed to bring luck in stag hunting. The dancers wear deer horns. Probably they used to wear a deerskin as well. Animal skins and horns were also worn in battle by warriors to give them the strength and cunning of beasts. The Vikings' horned helmets, the ocelot skins of Montezuma's soldiers and the bearskins of the British Guards all have their origins in this custom.

THE DRUIDS. Stonehenge is a circle of huge stones which lies on Salisury Plain in England. In ancient times, it was an important place for the Druids. They were sun worshippers, and these modern Druids are celebrating their main festival on Midsummer's Day. They carry banners with magical signs. For example, the banner on the left shows the sun. The huge boulders which form the temple at Stonehenge were used in astronomy. On Midsummer's Day the sun rises directly over the upright heelstone outside the monument.

BONFIRES. If you have stared into a flickering coal fire you will agree that the flames are both strange and magical. It has always been part of a sorceror's stock-in-trade to appear to master fire and use it as a source of magical energy. Bonfires give out light and warmth on a dark night. They are another form of magic used to bring back the sun. In England this form of *ritual* still survives in Guy Fawkes celebrations. Fire was also thought to purify and witches were often burnt at the stake.

CORN DOLLY. Corn was the main food of early agricultural peoples and spells were woven to make sure of a good harvest. In Britain, the last ears of corn were not cut. It was believed that the spirit of the corn lived in the last sheaf. The ears of corn were plaited into a "corn dolly" like the one shown here. This was then kept as a good-luck charm until the following season. In Cornwall, in the west of England, the last sheaf was always cut by the oldest reaper. It was then decorated with ribbons like the goddess it represented.

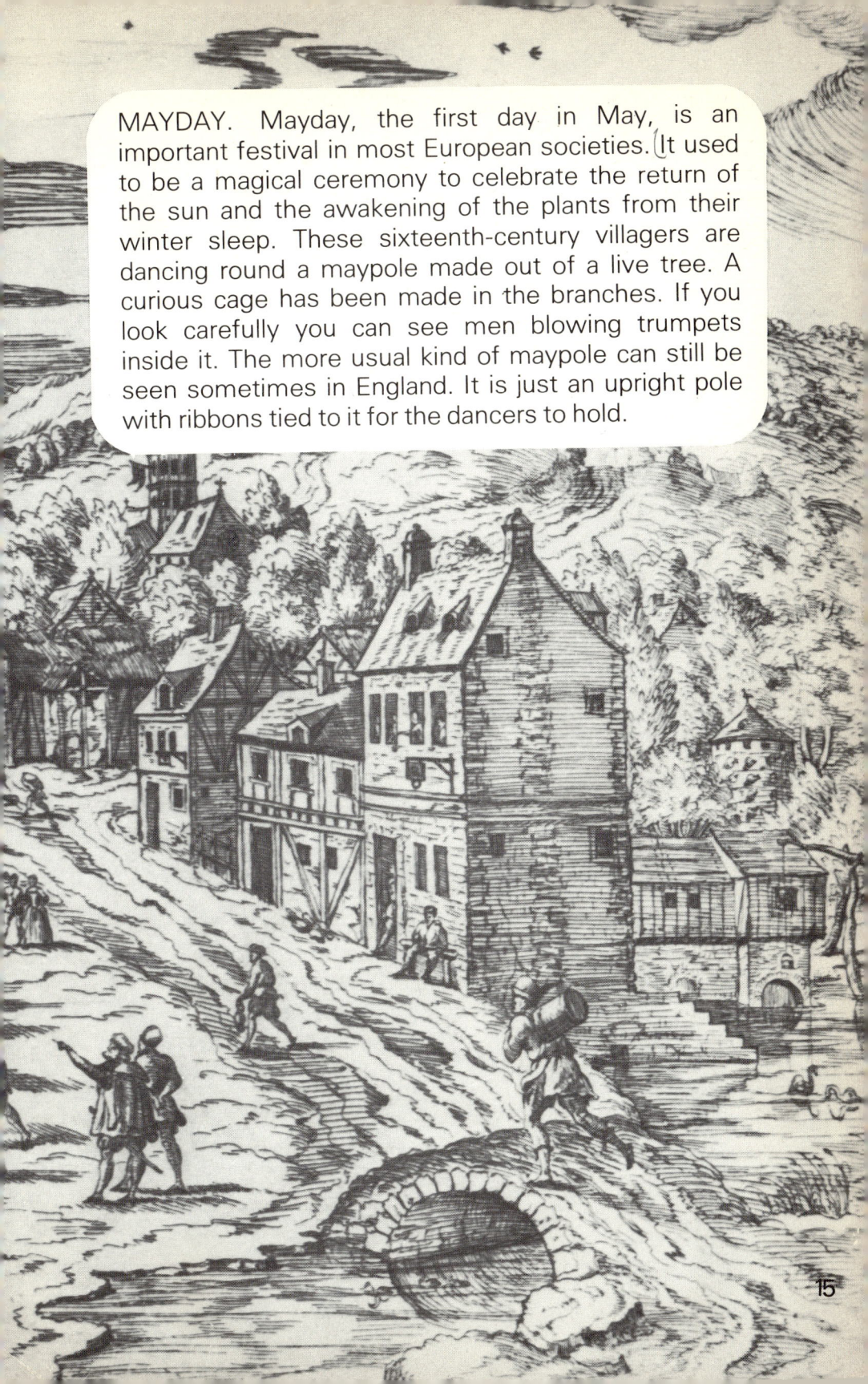

MAYDAY. Mayday, the first day in May, is an important festival in most European societies. It used to be a magical ceremony to celebrate the return of the sun and the awakening of the plants from their winter sleep. These sixteenth-century villagers are dancing round a maypole made out of a live tree. A curious cage has been made in the branches. If you look carefully you can see men blowing trumpets inside it. The more usual kind of maypole can still be seen sometimes in England. It is just an upright pole with ribbons tied to it for the dancers to hold.

HELSTON FURRY DANCE. Another magical *ritual* which still survives from the old Maytime festivities is the Helston Furry Dance. This is held every year on 8th May. Couples, dressed in white, dance in pairs through the streets of Helston in Cornwall to celebrate the spring. The word "Furry" comes from "Fer" which once meant fair. The festival may also be linked with the Roman flower goddess, Flora. Morris dancing, flower festivals, May fairs and madrigal singing on Mayday all have the same magical origins.

THE MOTHER GODDESS. Birth and *fertility* have always been surrounded by magical "old wives' tales". Early societies needed children to help with the hunting and farming. Fertility goddesses, like the one shown above, were brought gifts by childless women, or by those who wanted a safe birth. The figures were often ugly but their fatness must have been thought lucky by the primitive tribes. This statue is known as the Flint Goddess and comes from the prehistoric settlement at Grimes' Graves in England.

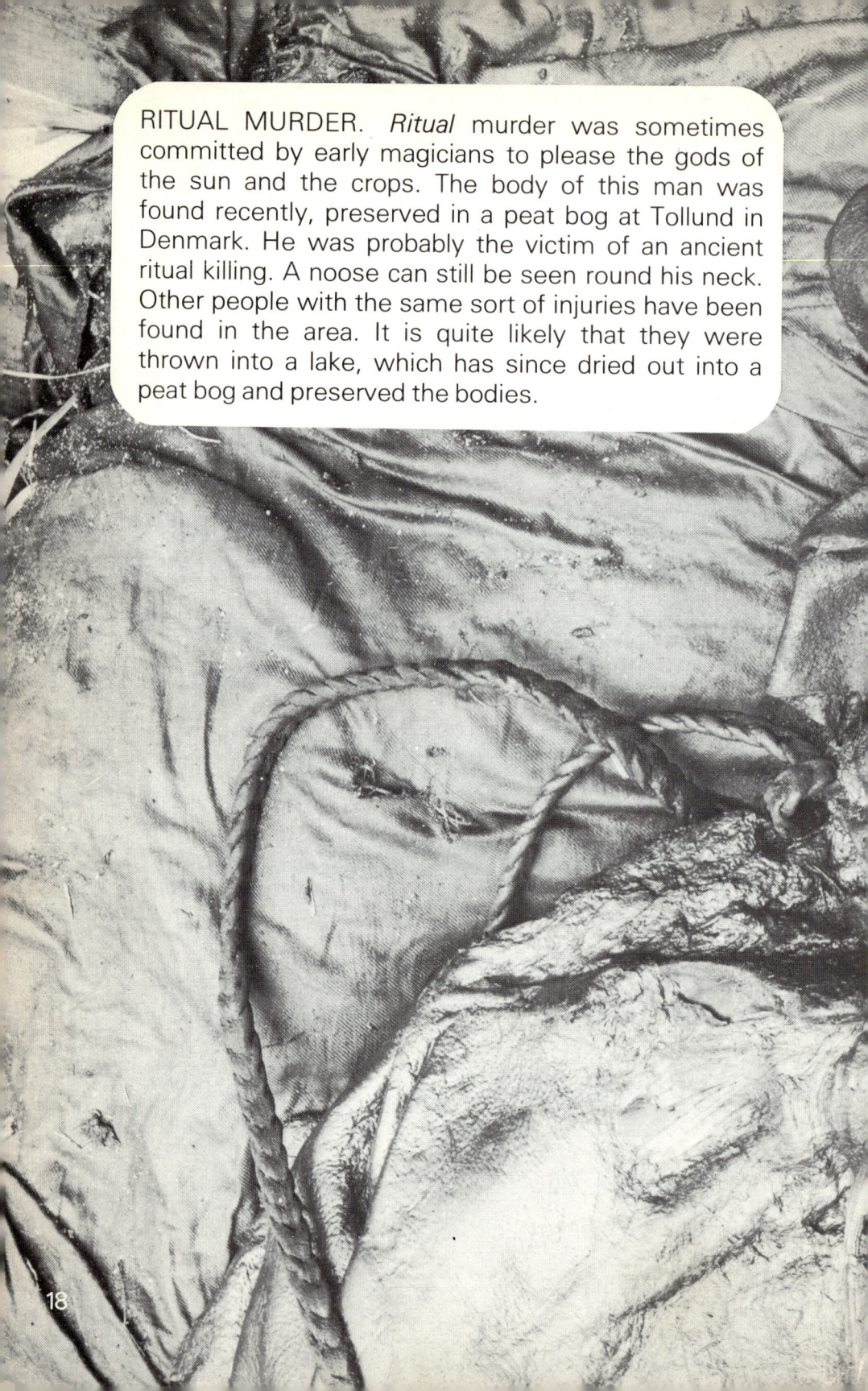

RITUAL MURDER. *Ritual* murder was sometimes committed by early magicians to please the gods of the sun and the crops. The body of this man was found recently, preserved in a peat bog at Tollund in Denmark. He was probably the victim of an ancient ritual killing. A noose can still be seen round his neck. Other people with the same sort of injuries have been found in the area. It is quite likely that they were thrown into a lake, which has since dried out into a peat bog and preserved the bodies.

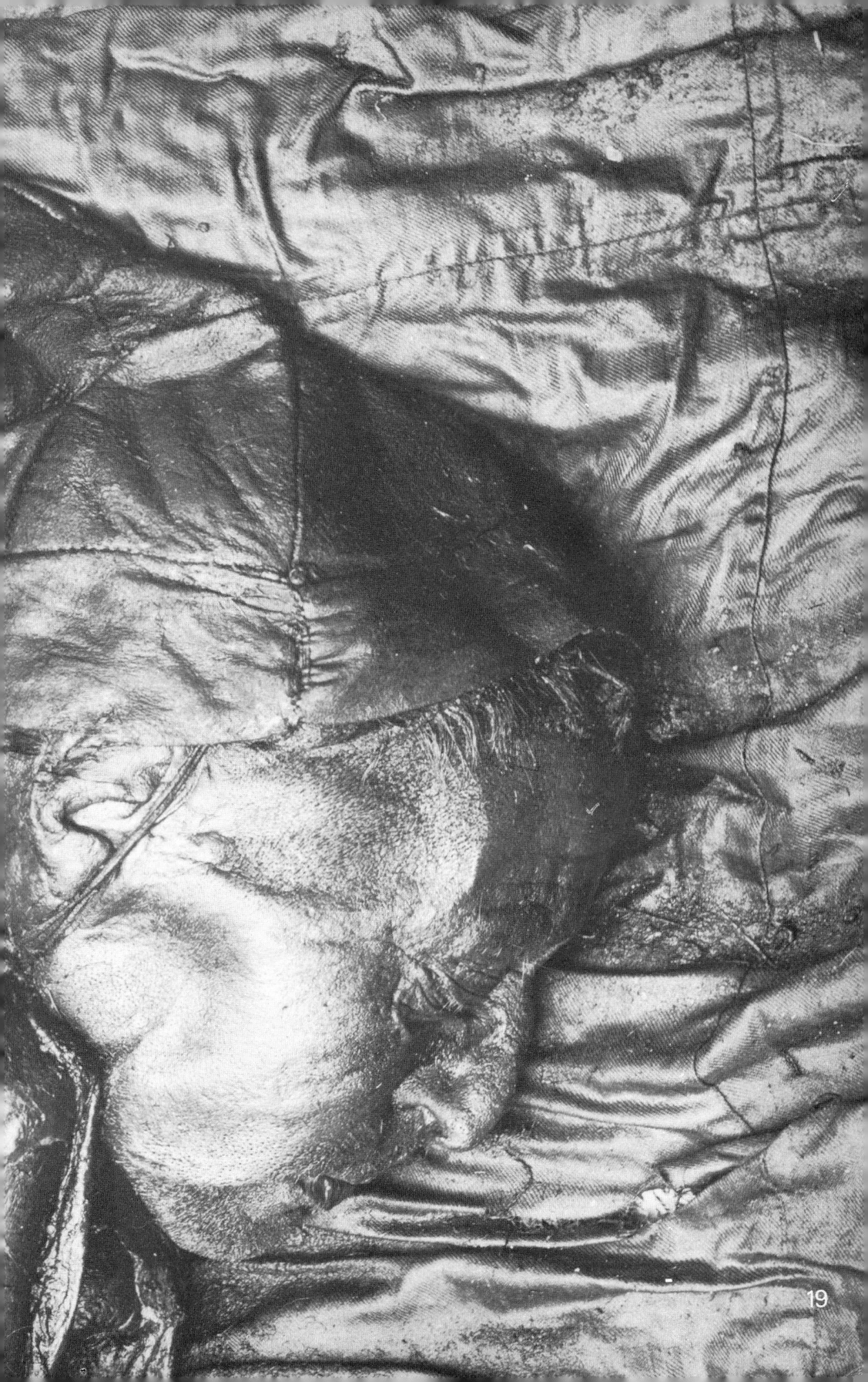

THE WICKER MAN. A scapegoat is an important part of magical practice. In the Old Testament a goat was sent out into the desert on the Day of Atonement bearing the sins of the people. According to Julius Caesar, the Druids sacrificed prisoners for the same reason. They were burned alive inside a giant wicker image. This frightening picture comes from the film *The Wicker Man*. You can just see the victim in the middle of the figure. The magicians believed that the sacrifice would persuade the gods to forget about the sins of the people.

MEDUSA. A magician's power depends on fear. Primitive people felt that it was easy to stir up the anger of the gods. They would try to avoid trouble whenever they could. This huge head of Medusa comes from the Greek temple at Didyma in Turkey. Medusa was a powerful magician. People turned to stone if they looked at her face. Perseus (a Greek hero) was able to kill her because he only looked at her reflection in his polished shield.

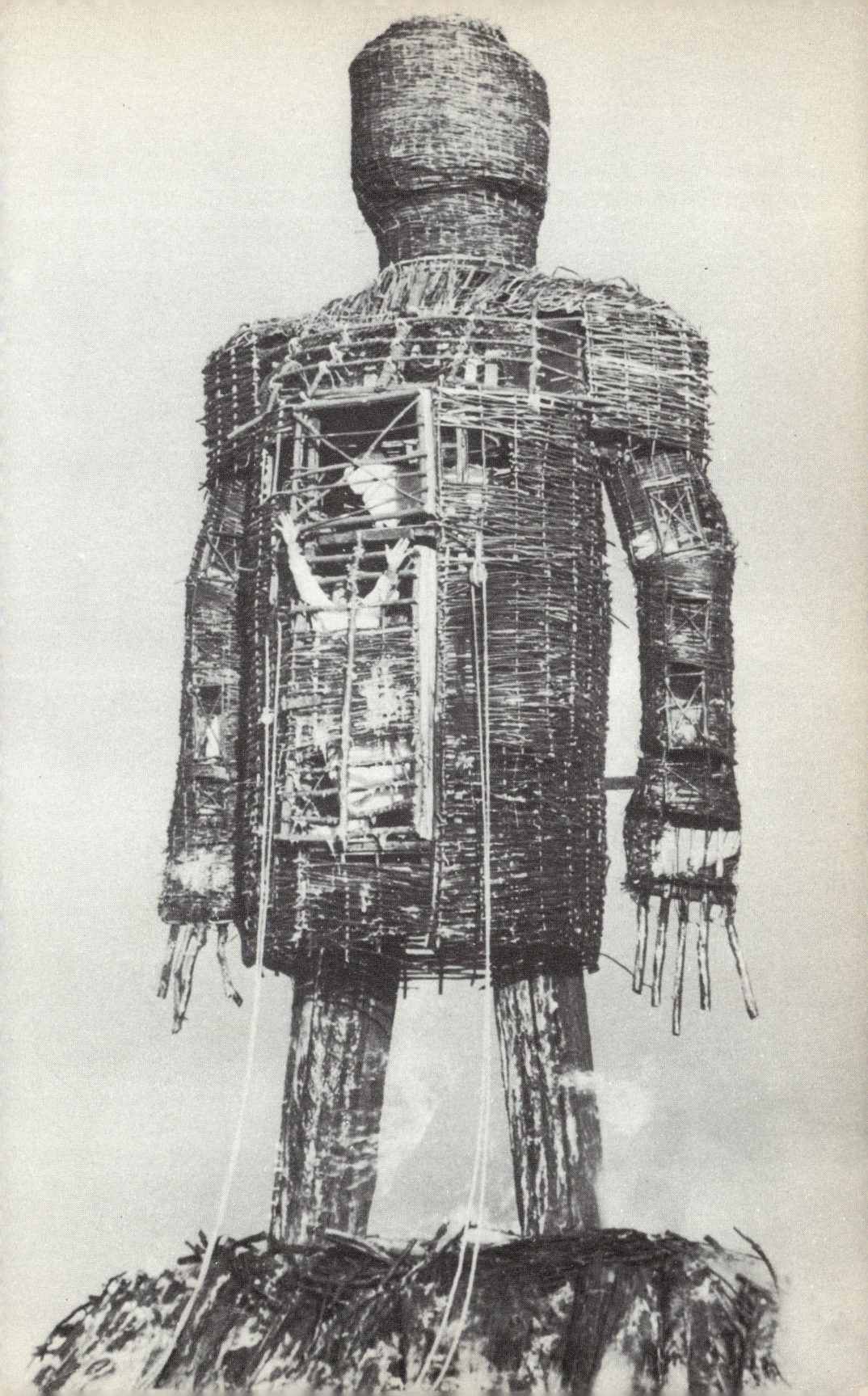

MASKS. Masks are very much part of *ritual* magic. They are still used by African magicians today. Masks change the wearers into different creatures. They have the freedom to behave as they want to, You can see this if you watch a carnival procession today. This is the mask of the spirit of the forest. It has horns to show that the spirit is an animal. The strange face and stripes of white paint are to frighten people.

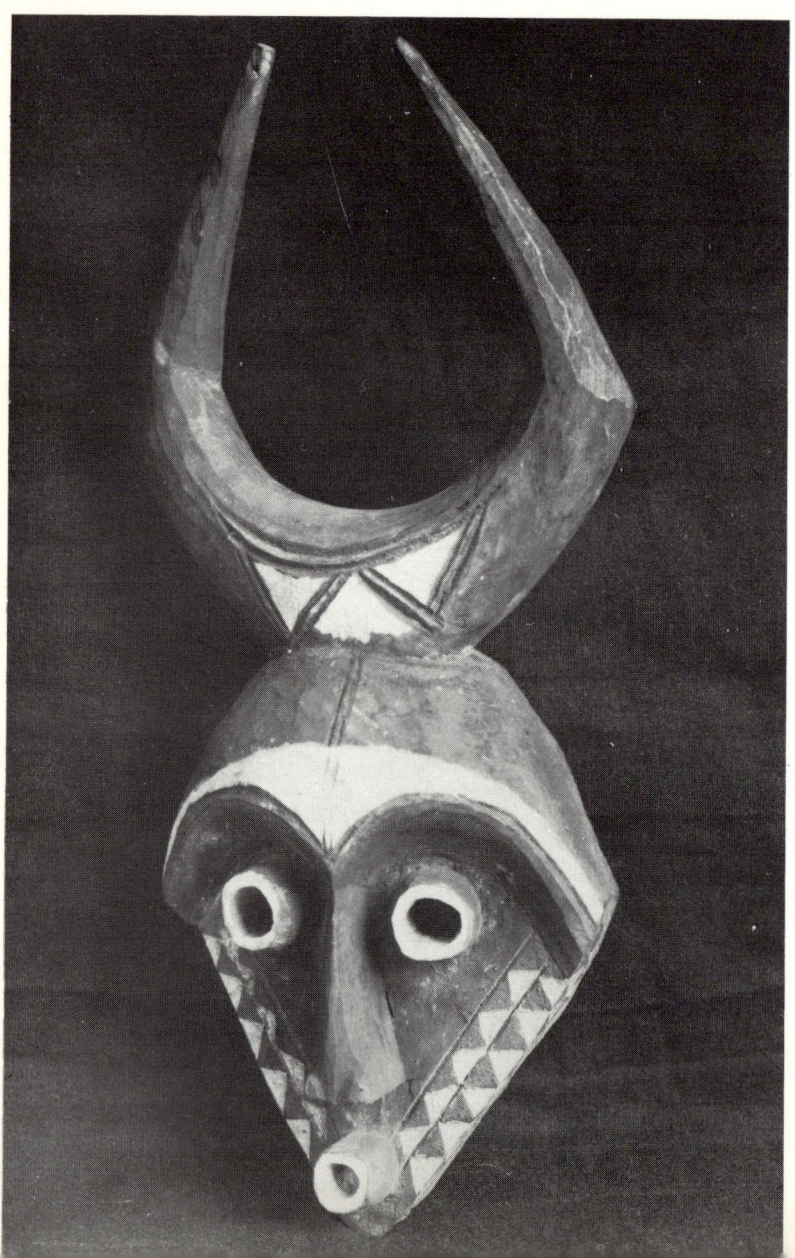

MAGICAL HAND. This Roman magical hand must have been a very powerful good-luck charm. A lucky pine-cone is balanced on the thumb and there is a snake ring on one finger. A ram's head and other magical signs are carved on the palm. Rings have always been magical and hand movements are often used in spells. We still keep the devil at bay by crossing our fingers. We are told not to point. This is not only because it is rude, but also because the index finger was once known as the witch's cursing finger.

THE SEA. Sailors have always been very superstitious. Ships' figureheads were believed to hold the soul of the ship. They were usually female in form and were always carefully looked after during a voyage. These figures come from a museum at Falmouth in Cornwall. When mounted on the prow (front) of a ship, they must have been an impressive sight. They were rather like goddesses looking out to sea.

LUCK. Horseshoes and horsebrasses are good-luck charms in many countries. Horseshoes are made of iron, which has always been a lucky metal. An old saying in Britain was, "Touch wood, no good. Touch iron, rely on". In the old stories, horses pulled the chariots of the gods. They are also thought to be magical. The horseshoe is in the shape of a crescent moon, which is another magical symbol. Some of the horseshoes in this collection at Oakham Castle date from the time of Queen Elizabeth I of England.

EASTER EGGS. These gaily-painted Easter eggs come from Czechoslovakia. They are a symbol of rebirth, or being born again. Once, they were linked with the pagan rites of spring. This is because plants were "reborn" at that time of the year. In parts of Europe scarlet eggs are still planted in the fields to protect the crops against storms. They are decorated because it was thought that the Virgin Mary dyed eggs to amuse the infant Jesus. This is one of the many occasions when magical pagan customs and Christian beliefs have joined together to make a new tradition.

2. Witches and Demons

When Christianity came, sorcerors lost their high position in the community. The early Christians believed in magic like the pagans but they did not approve of other religions. In 1485 Pope Innocent VIII declared that people had strayed from the Catholic faith and had begun to worship the Devil. Women were singled out for persecution for a variety of reasons. In the first place, they were thought more likely to keep faith with the old religion. What is more, some of the pagan beliefs focused on a mother goddess. Also the male priests hated and feared physical desire.

This nineteenth-century illustration is a good example of the Christian Devil that witches were believed to worship. He has the head and legs of a goat and large wings. He looks rather like the prehistoric magician who dressed in an animal skin and wore horns on his head. Between the fifteenth and seventeenth centuries many innocent women were put to death for being witches. Most of them were only following the magical practices that had been the custom for centuries.

DEMONS. After the coming of Christianity the gods of the pagans became classed as demons. Some of them have been resurrected as gargoyles. These are the strange stone figures round the roof tops of medieval churches and cathedrals. This is a fifteenth-century gargoyle from Winchcombe Parish Church in Gloucestershire, England. It is half-man and half-bird and snarls like a demon.

WAX IMAGES. Death was often sudden and terrible 500 years ago. Nobody knew much about disease. Death was often blamed on outsiders. Witches were believed to cause illness and death by making wax figures of their victims. The models were stuck full of pins or melted in front of the fire. This caused the person to sicken and die. In the picture below the Devil is giving wax figures to a group of witches. Nasty-looking creatures are flying in the air.

THE SABBAT. The medieval Christian Church believed that witches worshipped one Devil. He was the opposite, in every way, to the one God that Christians believed in. This engraving shows a witches' "church service", or *sabbat.* The witches (usually thirteen in number) dance round a giant Devil who is part goat and part man. He holds a mass candle in one hand and a witch's broomstick in the other. A familiar spirit looks on, with other strange creatures. It was believed the witches took part in a "black mass", their version of the Christian mass.

FLYING. Many people believed that witches flew to their meetings on broomsticks, using bats' blood as a flying ointment. Flying was one of the tests of a witch. In some witch trials the verdict was recorded: "Not guilty, no flying". Strangely enough, many witches on trial actually said that they could fly. Modern writers think that the witches rubbed themselves with an ointment containing aconite and belladonna, or took drugs before the sabbat. These drugs made them think that they were flying through the air, like the Indian magician on page 6. The sixteenth-century witch in the picture below is leaving

through the chimney. A suspicious man is looking through the keyhole.

MAGIC CIRCLE. This scene from the film *The Wicker Man* shows a modern witch using a magic circle to call up evil spirits. A circle has always been a strong magical symbol. The old *fertility* dances were performed in circles. Many of the witches of old were only trying to bring good fortune to the crops. In the foreground you can see a hobby horse. These are still used in carnivals. They survive from the days when magicians dressed up as animals.

RAIN-MAKING. We would all like to control the weather. Here two witches are brewing a storm. They are calling on the aid of a serpent and a cockerel which they are throwing into the flames. Rain-making was really good magic, but the medieval Church was against spells of all kinds. Witches were also believed to cause lightning. People thought that a building or tree struck by lightning would bear the marks of the Devil's claws and would smell of sulphur.

AGNES SAMPSON. Agnes Sampson and her coven (group) of witches worked with the Earl of Bothwell in 1590 to try to kill James I by witchcraft. First they tried to drown the king by causing a storm when he was at sea. When this failed, they tried making an image of him. Bothwell escaped when the plot was discovered but the witches confessed at their trial. Agnes Sampson, on the left of the group in this picture, was very proud of her powers as a witch. She told the king the exact words that he spoke to his queen on their wedding night. All the witches were put to death.

WHITE MAGIC. Many of those people accused of witchcraft actually practised good, or white, magic. Like this old witch, from the film *The Masque of the Red Death*, many were wise women of the village. They practised herbal magic and sold love charms. In the picture the witch is being given a magic rose by a hooded stranger which forecasts the coming of the plague to her village.

LOVE CHARMS. Finding a marriage partner is a very chancy business and love charms can still be bought today. This heart-shaped pin cushion was given to a sailor by his wife or sweetheart. It was supposed to keep him safe at sea, and to bring him back to her. It dates from the First World War and has British flags in the middle. The pins make a pretty pattern. The heart is an important magical symbol and many people own a heart-shaped locket or charm.

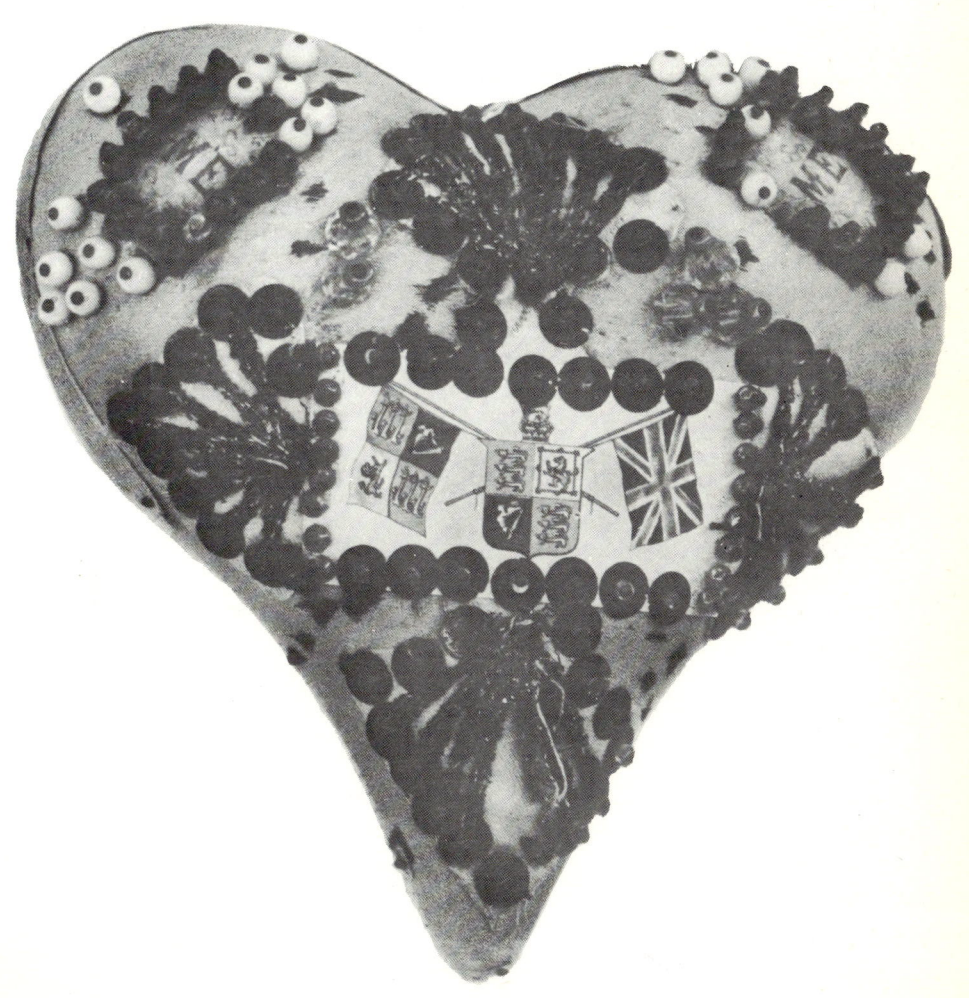

THE MANDRAKE. Anaesthetics are a recent discovery. In the past, herbs and roots like the mandrake were used for minor operations. The mandrake root, like the ginseng root today, was believed to have strange powers. It was a powerful anaesthetic and could be used to stop toothache and other sicknesses. Witches were supposed to gather it at night by tying a dog to the plant. The plant was said to give a dreadful shriek when uprooted. This would kill the dog when he heard it, and might otherwise have killed the witch. The root was shaped rather like a human figure, and this is why the medieval artist has drawn it this way.

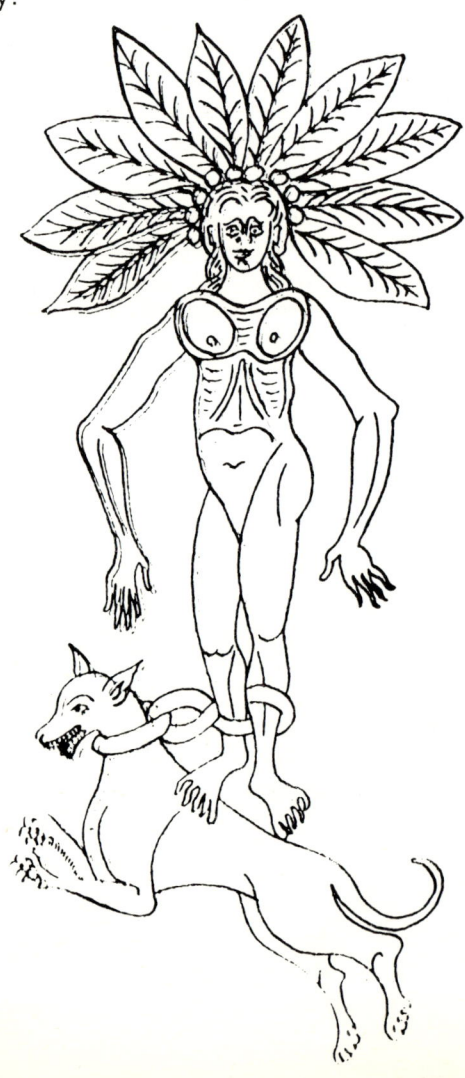

MATTHEW HOPKINS. No one knew for certain who was a witch. The famous seventeenth-century witch-finder, Matthew Hopkins, boasted that he could always get a conviction. He is shown here questioning one of the witches (on the right). She is giving him the names of her familiar spirits. Apart from "Vinegar Tom" in the foreground, most of them look like normal domestic pets. Sir John Holt is on the left. He was very much against the cruel methods that Hopkins used to get a confession.

SWIMMING A WITCH. One way of deciding whether a person was a witch was the practice of swimming. This was based on the old pagan custom of trial by water. If the sacred water rejected the body, and the witch floated, she was guilty. It was said that the Leicestershire witches of 1717 "swam like a cork, a piece of paper, or an empty barrel, though they strove all they could to sink". These witches look as if they are floating. Two familiar spirits are in the stream on the right and another is on the bank. The witch-finders

stand on the left. The cart in the background is waiting to take the witches to their deaths.

BURNING A WITCH. The worst place to live if you were a witch was Europe. There, the witches were burnt alive, like these three women who died at Derneburg in Germany in 1555. The Devil has appeared to the women in their last moments, in the form of a flying serpent. The witch-finders look on in the background.

PACT WITH THE DEVIL. This Victorian cartoon tries to make witchcraft into a bit of a joke. However, the real picture was not like this at all. The persecution of witches caused terrible cruelties. The witches themselves were believed to practise some awful rites. One of these was the pact with the Devil. The witch gave her soul to the Devil in exchange for magical powers. Anyone who has read the story of *Dr Faustus* will know that the Devil always came to collect what was owed to him. Here he is taking an unwilling witch off to Hell on his black horse.

BEWITCHING. The ill-wishing behind all black magic is chilling. The picture above is of a witch's cursing bone. It comes from Argyll, in Scotland, and is made out of bone and a piece of bog wood. The victims of spells believed in magic as much as the witches did. For this reason they could be "wished" into illness. The object below is a cow bewitcher. If a spell had been put on the animal, some of its milk had to be passed through the hole to cure it. The Horniman Museum in London has many examples of these strange rural charms.

AFRICAN WITCHCRAFT. Witchcraft is still practised in many countries today. In Africa the witch doctors are always men. Their magic is very similar to the witchcraft of sixteenth-century Europe. These two African tribesmen are trying to make rain. A black goat is killed. The stomach is then cut out and used for the *ritual*.

FETISH. This is a Nigerian fetish or good-luck charm. He looks very much like the Devil of the European witches. He has horns and looks as if he is wearing a mask. He is probably a hunting charm as he is playing a pipe. According to the old Nigerian stories, a piper always went with Sango, the hunter god, on a hunting expedition. The Yoruba tribe of Southern Nigeria believe that spirits haunt the world. These spirits live inside animals. They also have female witches who are believed to fly at night, like the European witches of old.

3. Looking into the Future

The basis of all black magic is that everything is pre-ordained. What this means is that all the things that happen to you in your life were decided before you were even born. The magician has only to find the right formula and all the world could be set to rights. Although people believed that their future was already decided for them, it could still be changed by good luck. Charms and spells could bring out the good things in a *horoscope* and take away the bad things. Even today people try not to "tempt fate", or be too optimistic. Perhaps they are afraid that this will make the gods change their minds.

The Greeks went to their state oracles to ask questions about public and private affairs. The oracle was a person who could speak on behalf of a god. He or she was the "voice" of a god on earth. The greatest of the oracles was at Delphi. This city was believed to be the centre of the world. As you can see from the photograph, it is still a wonderful place. The priestess went into a trance when she was telling the future. She did this by chewing laurel leaves and breathing drugged fumes. She was believed to be speaking to the god Apollo. What she said was often muddled up. Her last message, delivered in 362AD, has come down to us clearly: "Tell the king", the priestess said, "that the curiously-built temple has fallen to the ground, that bright Apollo no longer has a roof over his head, or prophetic laurel, or babbling spring. Yes, even the murmuring water has dried up".

HARUSPICY. One of the earliest, and more unpleasant, ways of telling the future was by studying the insides of a sacrificed animal. This was known as haruspicy. The Babylonians and Assyrians used livers to make their forecasts. The clay model above was used as a guide for would-be prophets. The liver has been marked off in sections, and different *omens* written on each part. The Roman priests who told the future by this method were known as augurs.

ALECTOROMANCY. Another method used by the Romans for telling the future was alectoromancy. This was done by scattering grains of corn inside a circle made up of letters of the alphabet. Then a chicken was placed inside to pick out different letters. The method cannot have been very accurate. No doubt the priests would try to cheat by persuading the fowl to go in the right direction. The priests used a book to explain the message. This book can be seen in the middle background of the picture.

ASTROLOGY. Astrology is the art of telling fortunes by studying the stars. Astronomy is the science of studying the stars themselves. In ancient Egypt, astrology was thought to be as important a science as astronomy. The Egyptians mapped out the stars. Then they divided the year under *zodiac* symbols and made up a 365-day calender. In the picture the magical zodiac symbols are watching over the body of Sethi I in his tomb at Thebes in Egypt. Some of the signs shown here, like the lion and the bull, also have a place in a modern zodiac. The hippo-crocodile goddess Taurt is on the right. In front of her, the god Horus has a magical line which joins him to Apis the bull.

THE HOROSCOPE. The woman in the middle of this picture is giving birth to a baby. Meanwhile astrologers at the back of the room are casting a *horoscope* for the child. The exact time and place of birth are needed. Then the horoscope is worked out according to the exact position of the sun, moon and planets at this time. Astrologers could not be very precise before the invention of the telescope in 1610. These astrologers have no instruments to help them at all.

MEXICAN CALENDAR STONE. The Aztec kings of Mexico had to be astrologers as well as rulers. They were trained to study the stars and to give regular forecasts. This calendar stone stood at the top of the stairs in Montezuma's palace at Cactus Rock. The sun god is in the middle. Around him are signs that foretell the end of the present world in an earthquake. Symbols of the *zodiac* and the days are in the outer circle.

OMENS IN THE SKY. Even today an eclipse of the sun, a comet or a meteor can be quite frightening. They were once thought to be *omens* of disaster. A comet was seen in the sky before the Norman invasion of England in 1066. Here you can see a group of people watching the comet in a scene from the Bayeux Tapestry. After the battle the English said that they had known that it was a bad omen. For the Normans, of course, it was a lucky sign.

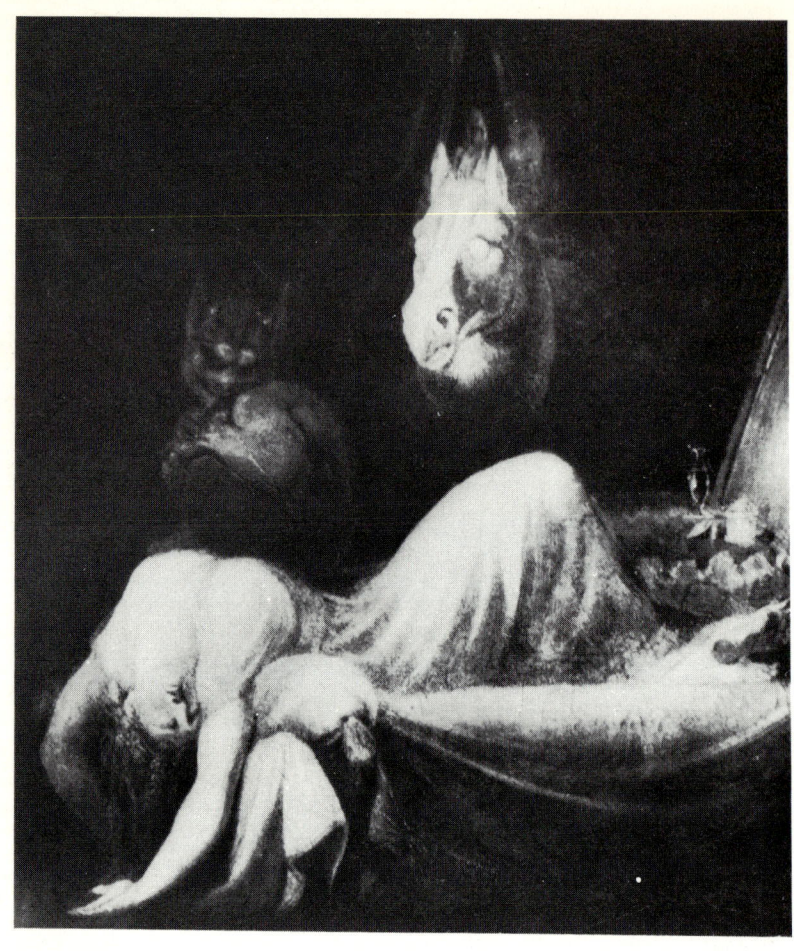

DREAMS. In early times dreams were used to foretell the future. The ancient Assyrians used a special *Dream Book* and in the Old Testament God spoke to his prophets in dreams. This painting by Fuseli is called *The Nightmare*. It shows the strange feelings we have when we dream. Dreams are not a very good way of foretelling the future but they do give an interesting look into how the dreamer is thinking and feeling.

I CHING. The Chinese still use a method of fortune-telling called I Ching. It is based on a book written by King Wen about a thousand years before the birth of Christ. It is based on two opposing forces. These are the forces of light and dark, positive and negative, which are called Yang and Yin. This nineteenth-century astrologer will give forecasts for a small fee. To do this he uses sticks. These are shown in the box at the front of the table. He makes calculations with them and looks up the results in the book of I Ching on the right.

PYROMANCY. In this picture the witch Ann Bodenham is foretelling the future from a pot of burning coals, on which imps are dancing. This practice is known today as pyromancy. It is the art of making deductions from the way a fire burns after certain herbs have been thrown on it. Another similar way of telling the future is to watch the flames of an oil lamp and see which way they move in a draught.

NOSTRADAMUS. Nostradamus was a famous sixteenth-century magician who looked into the future with the aid of a magic mirror. In the picture above, the French Queen Catherine de Medici is gazing into Nostradamus's mirror. It foretells the death of her husband Henry II. The magician is crouched inside a magic circle. In 1555 Nostradamus published a book of prophecies. In it he forecast the French Revolution, the death of Charles I and the rise of Hitler, among other events. His next forecast is for July 1999 when he says: "a great king of terror will descend from the skies . . .".

OLD MOTHER SHIPTON. Mother Shipton was an imaginary prophetess. Her forecasts appeared in nineteenth-century magazines. Here she looks rather like a witch, and her carriage is drawn by reindeer. She is supposed to have foretold the invention of the motor car. One of the old magazines, called *Old Moore's Almanac,* still publishes *horoscopes* today. Most long-range fortune-telling has now become rather like long-range weather forecasting: not very accurate and always a bit disappointing.

CHIROMANCY. Chiromancy or palmistry is fortune-telling by reading the lines on the palm of the hand. It has been practised since ancient times. Modern palmistry is usually done by gypsies. The art is based on the idea that the lines will have some effect on character and ability. In the picture opposite, the lifeline curves round the ball of the thumb, the heart line runs from the side of the hand to the middle. The other strongly-marked line in the picture is the head line.

CARTOMANCY. One of the most popular methods of fortune-telling is with playing cards, particularly with *tarot* cards. This old woman has laid the cards down on the floor and is reading the girl's fortune. There are many different methods of arranging the cards. Their purpose is to give ideas to the fortune-teller. Cards are often used for making prophecies about love. We still use the phrase, "lucky in cards, unlucky in love".

TEA LEAVES. The variety of different things that fortune-tellers read is endless. Even tea leaves were read, before the days of tea bags. This was usually done by amateurs. Forecasts are made from the patterns which the leaves make in the bottom of the cup after the tea has been drunk. The fortune-teller in this picture looks like a gypsy.

SCRYING. One of the oldest ways of looking into the future is by gazing into a shiny surface and reading the shapes. Crystal balls, mirrors and water have all been used. This is known as scrying, and is still used by fortune-tellers today. The crystal ball used by the famous Elizabethan magician, Dr John Dee, (see page 76) can still be seen at the British Museum.

4. Raising the Dead

Death is the greatest challenge of all for a magician. Most of the great civilizations believed in life after death. Some of the earliest magical practices were to do with burial customs. The royal cemetery at Ur, in the Middle East, dates from about 2500 BC. Here servants and soldiers were killed so that they could go into the afterlife with their masters. The ancient Egyptians used to *mummify* the bodies of people and animals when they died. In this way it was believed that the people would be able to carry on their normal lives in the world of the dead.

This picture was taken inside the tomb of Sen-Nufer at Thebes in Egypt. The tomb contained his mummified body. Round the walls the paintings show his life on earth. The king and queen are praying. The queen has a magical cross, the ankh, on her arm. The ankh is the sign of everlasting life. Grape vines are painted growing up the walls and over the ceiling which is just out of sight. Magical writings are on the walls of the tomb and on the case and wrappings of the mummy.

THE PYRAMIDS. The pyramids of Egypt are tombs for the *mummified* bodies of the earliest Egyptian pharaohs. Recent research suggests that the pyramid shape has some strange effects on the bodies inside it. It also helps the mummification process. The pyramids have always fascinated people. They formed the basis of some magical cults during the nineteenth and early twentieth centuries.

ORPHEUS AND EURYDICE. In primitive societies, a magician was believed to be able to slip across the boundary between life and death. Orpheus was a Greek magician and musician, who was supposed to have learnt his magic in Egypt. He journeyed to the Underworld to rescue his wife Eurydice. Part of the magic *ritual* was that he should not look back as he made the return journey. He did so and lost Eurydice.

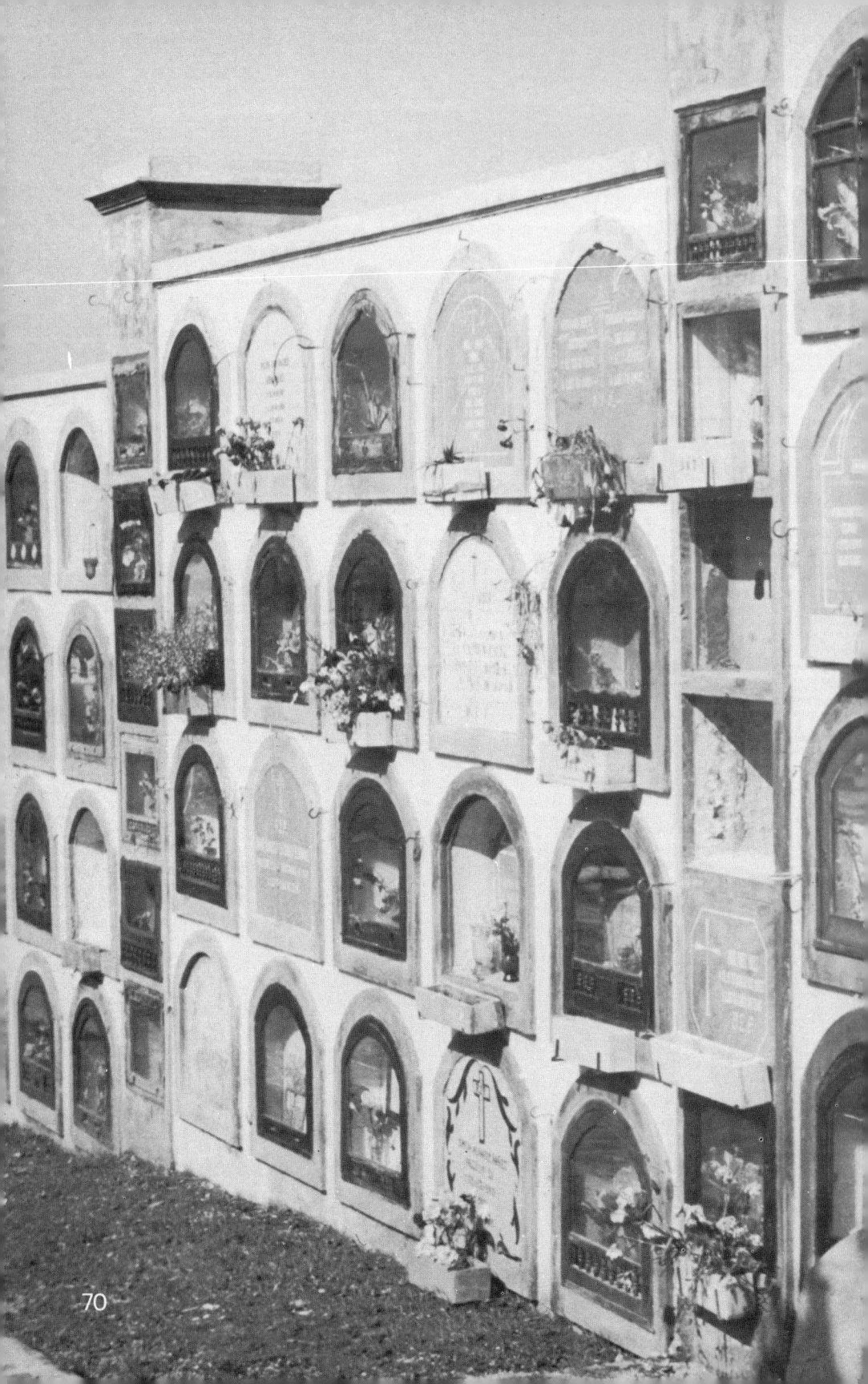

GRAVEYARD IN TENERIFE. This graveyard in Tenerife, in the Canary Islands, has small shrines for each body. The shrines are arranged like miniature villages in memory of the dead. Flowers, photographs and other mementos are put into the glass-fronted memorials. Laying flowers on a grave comes from the belief that the dead do not like to be forgotten. A wreath was once a magic symbol to enclose the soul of the dead person. In many countries relatives go to graveyards like this one to spend the day there and talk to the dead.

THE MEXICAN DEATH GOD. Many of the old magical customs to do with the dead are still practised in Mexico today. This rock crystal skull shows the Aztec god of death. All Souls' Day is called the Day of the Dead in Mexico. On this day it is the custom to sell figures, toys, cakes and sweets in the shape of skeletons in memory of dead relations. This survives from the pagan *ritual* of leaving food for the dead to keep them happy.

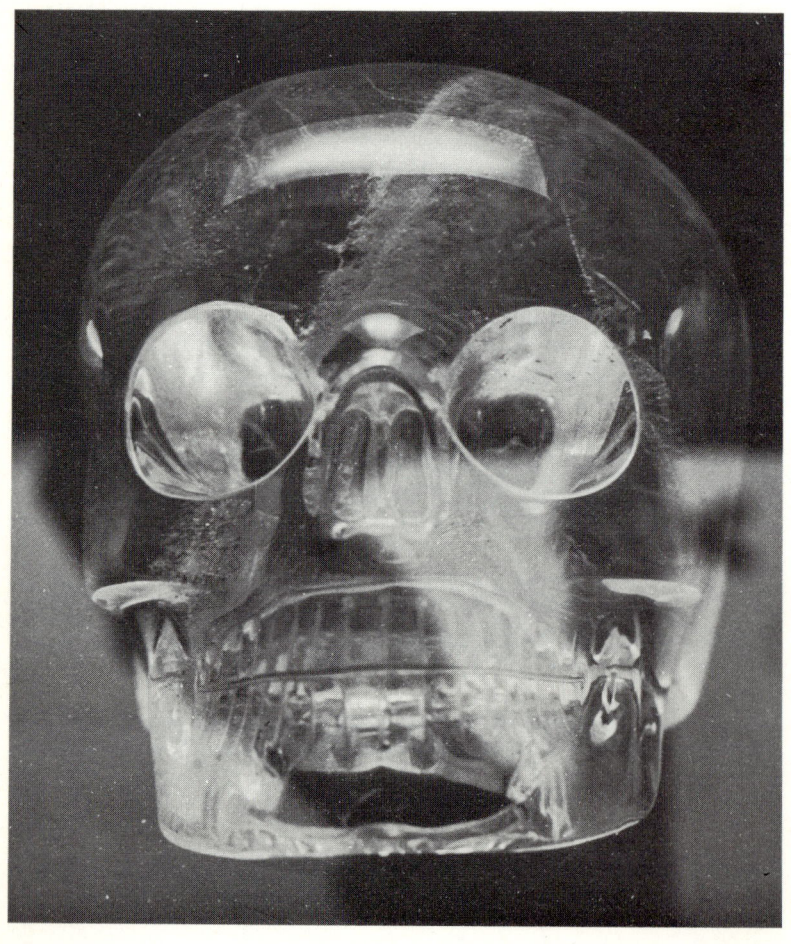

HALLOWE'EN. In Britain and in America the festival of Hallowe'en is celebrated. Its origins lie in the old pagan fire festival of Samhain and it is the night when ghosts walk. Hallowe'en is on 31st October, the day before All Souls' Day. On this night the dead were believed to return to their old homes to warm themselves in front of the fire. It was also a witch's festival. Today we try to frighten ourselves with masks and turnip lanterns in memory of the witches and ghosts of old.

NECROMANCY. Necromancy is fortune-telling by talking with the dead. In the Old Testament, King Saul went to the Witch of Endor for advice. The witch called up the prophet Samuel. In the picture, King Saul can be seen falling back in alarm at the vision. Saul was in fact breaking the Hebrew law by going to a witch for advice. The ghost of Samuel was angry at the king for disturbing him. He told Saul that the Israelites would be defeated the next day—and they were.

BANQUO'S GHOST. Witches were supposed to be able to raise the dead. The scene in this picture is from Shakespeare's play *Macbeth*. Three witches have called up the ghosts of eight Scottish kings. The last ghost is Banquo, whom Macbeth murdered. Shakespeare has given us the formula that the witches used for raising the ghosts. It contains lots of unpleasant things like "gall of goat, eye of newt, toe of frog, wool of bat and adder's fork".

DR DEE AND EDWARD KELLY. Dr John Dee (see page 64) was a famous sixteenth-century magician who was an alchemist. He also cast *horoscopes* for Queen Mary and Queen Elizabeth I. Unfortunately he became a friend of Edward Kelly who wanted to raise spirits. Here the two magicians have raised a rather angry-looking ghost in a cemetery. The two men are standing inside a circle which is meant to protect then from harm by the ghost.

PROTECTIVE SPIRIT. This wooden image is a protective spirit. The spirit world is still very real to the people of African tribes. Families often own a number of fetishes (good-luck charms) like this one to keep them safe. The image has a top hat on. Perhaps this means that it represents a very powerful ghost.

THE ANGELS OF MONS. Soldiers often tell stories of ghosts helping them fight wartime battles. During the First World War there was a report that angels appeared in the sky during the British retreat from Mons. Other soldiers reported that ghostly archers, like the ones in this picture, had protected them. Ghosts and battlefields often seem to go together. This is probably because most cultures believe that those who have not had a proper burial will return and haunt the place where they died. Few soldiers that die in battle ever get a proper burial.

BORLEY RECTORY. We still sometimes hear about houses which are supposed to be haunted. This picture is of Borley Rectory which was famous in the nineteen-thirties for ghostly goings-on. The house was built in 1863, but it was not until 1929 that ghosts started to appear. Here, investigators are searching for the skeleton of the phantom nun. Harry Price, the famous ghost-hunter, looked into the hauntings. He believed that many of the happenings could not be explained. The house has now been pulled down.

TABLE-TURNING. *Spiritualism* is the nineteenth and twentieth-century way of "talking" to the dead. The movement started in America with the Fox sisters. They are seated in the front of the picture and were only twelve and fifteen at the time. The sisters seemed to be mediums. A medium is a person through whom the spirits talk to the living. Here a table has risen into the air, much to the surprise of everyone. Another medium, Daniel Douglas Home, once caused a grand piano to rise into the air while the pianist was playing it!

SEANCES. *Spiritualist seances,* or meetings, became very popular in Victorian England. The most usual way for the spirit to pass its message was by rapping on a table. A group of people like this would sit round a polished table with their hands flat on the surface. Their fingers and thumbs would touch to make a complete circle. The spirit would answer questions, giving one rap for "no" and two raps for "yes". Another popular way of getting in touch was for everyone to place a finger on a wine glass in the middle of an alphabet circle. They would then record the letters as the glass moved towards them and make up words. This is quite similar to alectoromancy described on page 51.

MUSICAL SPIRITS. This nineteenth-century cartoon makes fun of *spiritualism*. At some *seances* the spirits communicated by playing musical instruments. An American called Mr Koons used to play the violin before a seance. Other ghostly instruments would take up the tune until it seemed as if a full orchestra was playing. The cartoonist was obviously an unbeliever when he shows this family at dinner, entertained by a strange, heavenly orchestra.

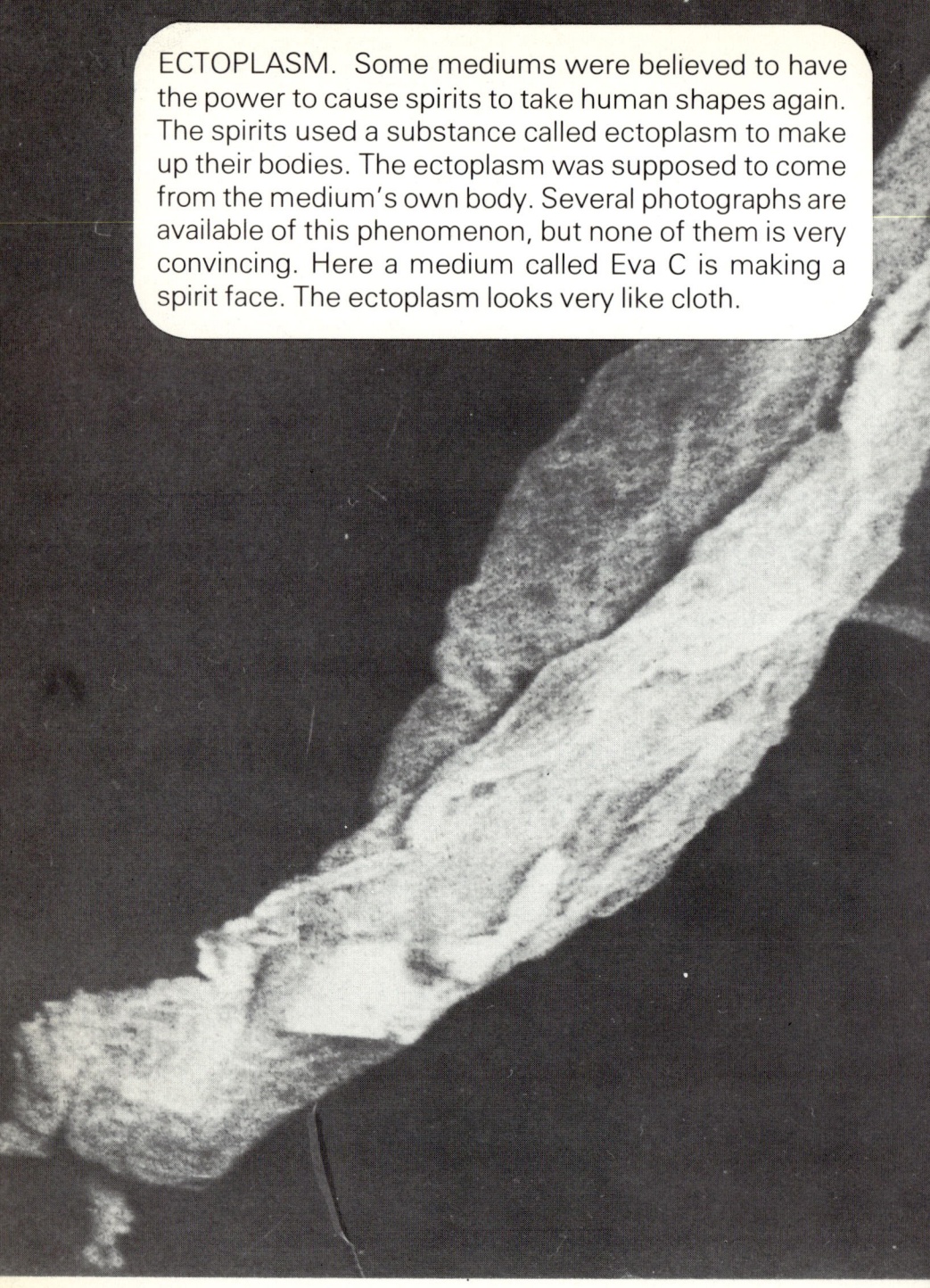

ECTOPLASM. Some mediums were believed to have the power to cause spirits to take human shapes again. The spirits used a substance called ectoplasm to make up their bodies. The ectoplasm was supposed to come from the medium's own body. Several photographs are available of this phenomenon, but none of them is very convincing. Here a medium called Eva C is making a spirit face. The ectoplasm looks very like cloth.

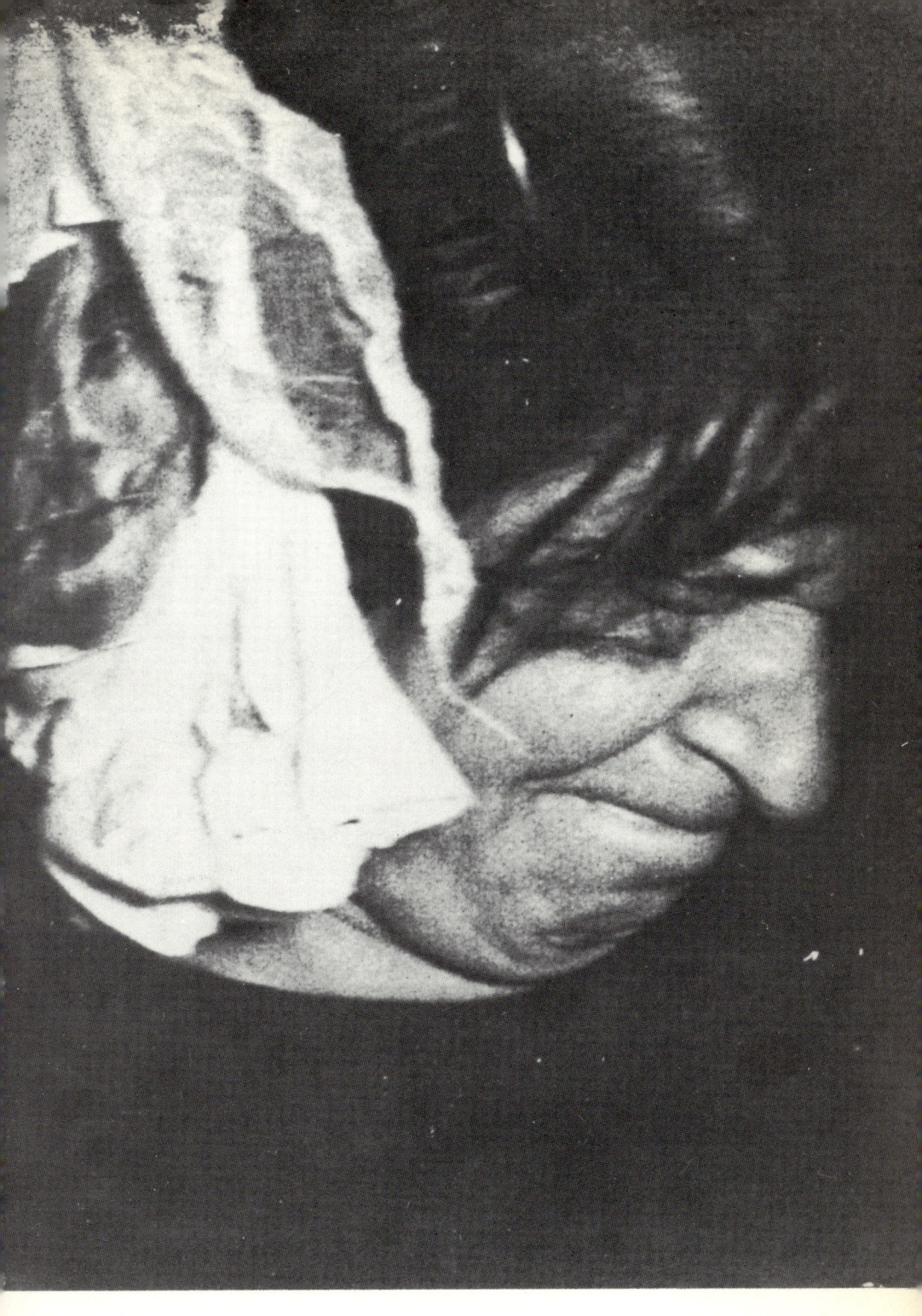

CHEATING MEDIUMS. A famous medium called Dr Slade was accused of taking money on false pretences by saying he was in touch with spirits. This engraving from the *Illustrated London News* shows Slade's trial in 1876. The famous stage illusionist, Maskelyne, is in the dock. He is showing that he could make writing appear on a slate by means of a simple conjuring trick. Slade insisted that spirits were doing the writing.

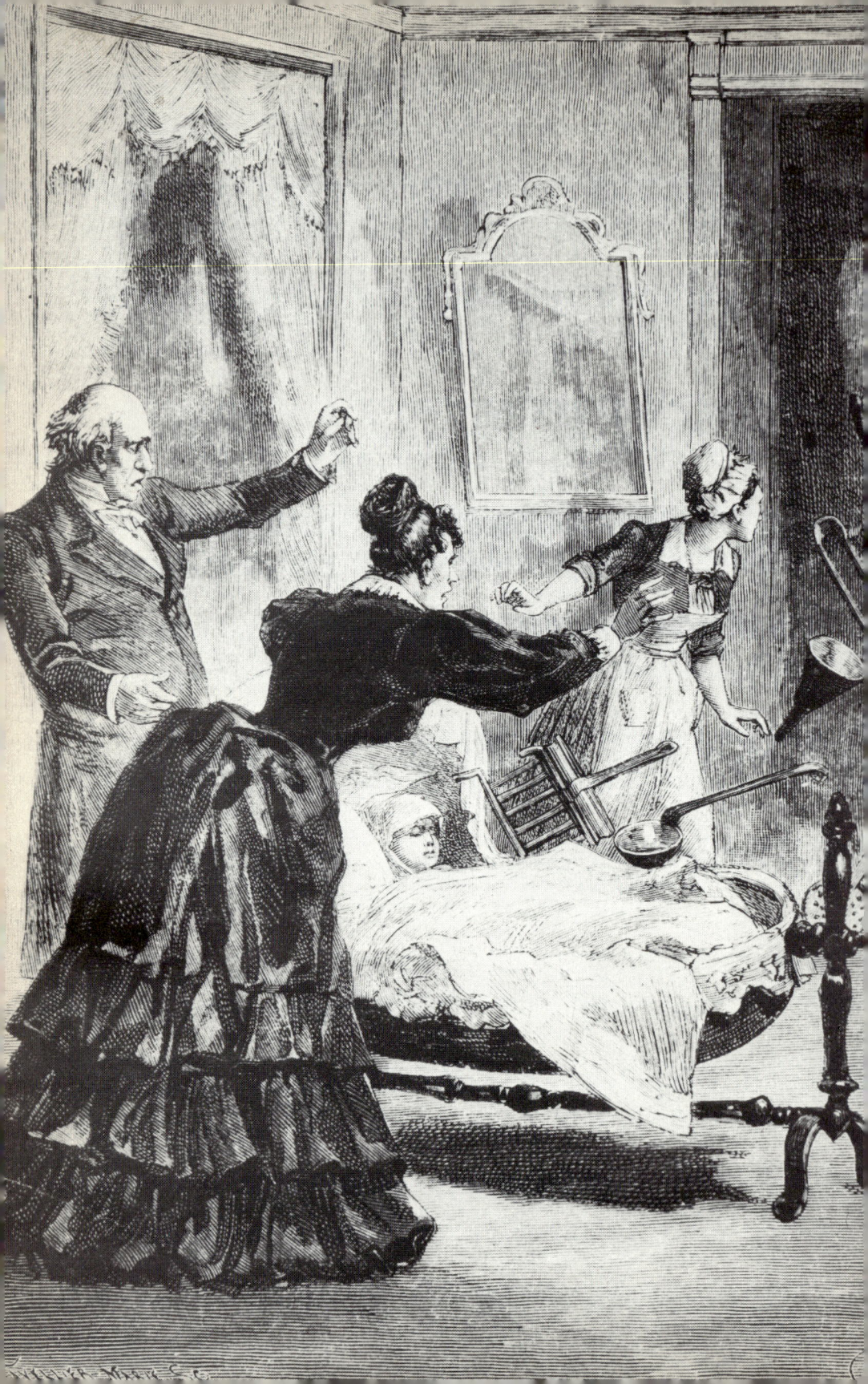

New Words

Astral	To do with the stars.
Cartomancy	Fortune-telling using playing cards.
Divining	Foretelling the future.
Fertility	Fruitfulness. The ability of plants and animals to grow and multiply.
Horoscope	Forecast of a person's future made by studying the planets and stars at the time of his birth.
Mummy	A human body preserved in wrappings by the ancient Egyptians.
Mysticism	Seeking direct communication with God or the gods.
Omens	Signs.
Reincarnation	Being born again in another form or body.
Ritual	A ceremony.
Sabbat	A witches' meeting.
Seance	Meeting when spiritualists try to contact the dead.
Spiritualism	Movement begun in the nineteenth-century to study communication with the dead.
Supernatural	Miraculous, magical.
Tarot	Special pack of playing cards used in fortune-telling.
Zodiac	Twelve sections marked on a map of the stars and planets, each with a different sign. The map is used to make out a person's horoscope.

More Books

Bessy, Maurice. *A Pictorial History of Magic and Superstition* (Spring Books 1961).
Briggs, Katherine. *A Dictionary of Fairies* (Penguin 1977).
Dickinson, Peter, *Chance, Luck and Destiny* (Penguin 1976).
Dickinson, Susan. *Ghostly Encounters* (Fontana 1970).
Encyclopedia of Magic and Superstition (Octopus).
Green, Andrew. *Ghost Hunting — A practical guide* (Mayflower 1973).
Hart, Roger. *Witchcraft* (Wayland 1973).
Hole, Christina. *Witchcraft in England* (Batsford).
James, M.R. *Collected Ghost Stories.*
Renault, Mary. *The King Must Die* (Longman 1958).

Index

Alchemy 27
Alectoromancy 51
Astrology 11, 52, 53, 54, 57
Astronomy 52

Bogies 79

Cartomancy 63
Charms 7, 12, 23, 38, 46, 49, 81
   horseshoes 25
   love 39
Corn dollies 12
Crowley, Aleister 91

Dee, Dr John 64, 76
Demons 29, 30
Devil 29, 30, 32-3, 43, 44
Dreams 56
Druids 11, 20

Easter eggs 26
Ectoplasm 86

Familiar spirits 32, 41
Dr Faustus 44
Fertility 9, 17

Fetishes 46
Fire 12
Flying saucers 92
Fortune-telling 52, 57, 60, 63, 64, 74

Ghosts 76, 78, 79, 81, 82

Hallowe'en 73
Haruspicy 50
Helston Furry Dance 16
Herne the Hunter 77
Hopkins, Matthew 41
Horn Dance 8
Horoscopes 7, 53, 60, 76

I Ching 57

Macbeth 74
Magic circles 35
Mandrake 40
Mascots 7
Masks 22
Mayday 15
Mediums 83, 86, 89
Medusa 20

Necromancy 74

Nostradamus 59

Omens 50, 54
Oracles 49

Palmistry 60
Phrenology 62
Poltergeists 91
Pyramids 68
Pyromancy 58

Rain-making 36
Rituals 7-27, 68
Black Sabbat 33
Sampson, Agnes 37
Scapegoats 20
Scrying 64

Spells 7, 23, 45, 49
Spiritualism 83, 84, 85
Sun worship 10, 11

Tarot cards 63
Tollund man 18-19

Witches 29-47, 58
   African 46
   and the Church 29, 33
   and the Devil 32, 33, 44
   and flying 34-5
   their magic 30, 36, 38, 45
   their persecution 34, 37, 41, 42-3
White magic 38

Picture Credits

The author and publishers wish to thank the following for the pictures which appear in this book:

British Lion Ltd, 21, 35; British Museum, 17, 22, 23, 47, 58, 69, 80; British Tourist Authority, 9, 11, 16, 25, 31; Dover Publications Ltd, 28; EMI, 38; Mary Evans 75, 83, 86-7, 90, 92; Pat Hodgson, 8, 20, 24, 40, 43, 48, 52, 66, 70-1, 77, 78, 79, 85; R C Lambeth (Shire Publications), 12; Radio Times Hulton Picture Library, *Frontispiece,* 10, 13, 46, 50, 51, 54, 56, 57, 59, 60, 62, 64, 68, 72, 73, 74, 76, 81, 82, 84, 91; Victoria and Albert Museum, 14-15, 44; Wayland Picture Library, 6, 18-19, 26, 27, 30, 32, 33, 34, 36, 37, 39, 41, 42, 45 (top and bottom), 53, 55, 61, 88-9.

WITHDRAWN

WITHDRAWN

DATE DUE

133.4
Hod

34529

Hodgson, Pat
  Witchcraft and magic

1/06 pgs missing 9, 10, 27-28, 31, 32
61, 62 77, 78, 80, 91, 92